# ULTIMATE
# INSPIRATION

## POWER OF POSITIVE YOU

DR. ROBERT SCOTT

ISBN 978-0-9847119-9-4

WWW.ROBERTSCOTT.US.COM

© 2015 ROBERT SCOTT

# TABLE OF CONTENTS

**Part I – Discovering Your Truth**

**Part II – Creating Your Vision**

**Part III – Establishing Your Legacy**

Part I

# Discovering Your Truth

# 1.

# Inner Wisdom

How do you live a good life? A life that is filled with joy, love and personal satisfaction that expresses the unique gift that each and every one of us were given to develop to its ultimate potential.

It's all a matter of such simple choices that we make every day and an understanding of how your gift will bring its unique contribution to this complex world where we all live.

The place to begin is with your understanding about **Energy**. This is your *internal energy* that comes from your **Spirit** and your **Mind**. This is the place where you pull all the elements of Self together or you do not. Everything in your life is about your ability to effectively manage your *energy, spirit and mind*.

Positive, healthy individuals know the rhythm of their mind and body. They have an active internal life which nurtures their spirit, mind and body on a continuous basis.

They actively advance positive thoughts and resist negative energies that they encounter daily from a diverse group of external sources.

Through *Positive Self Talk* they form a core of resiliency which is reinforced through healthy life choices that work together and from these collective successful experiences form a positive lynchpin that only grows in its strength the more it is used. The critical factor is having a vibrant *Inner Life* either by spiritual beliefs or humanistic philosophies —for these are *Altruistic Energies*.

Along with this is a compass, road map and gas card in the form of your *Life Ethic, Guiding Logic & Compelling Passion*. This handy trio helps set the course for your journey but more importantly keeps it on course and sustains its ever advancing progress to its final destination. Yet the greatest learning is not found at the final destination but on your journey of *Self- Discovery* and *Self-Knowledge..* this is where you will find *Your Truth* and how it relates to your *Inner Wisdom*.

With these basic frameworks in place you have created the core of your Inner Wisdom that is established with your **Five Focal Facts**.

| | |
|---|---|
| **Believe in Your Truth:** | What makes you, you? |
| **Define Your Vision:** | Where do you want to go with it? |
| **Perpetuate Your Brand:** | How do you express what you believe? |
| **Inspire with Your Zeal:** | How will you bring others on your journey? |
| **Establish Your Legacy:** | What will remain from your efforts? |

These are your vision statements and operating manual that define the life objectives which you seek to achieve.

Honestly answering these questions is a big step forward in becoming **Authentic**. Your *Authenticity* is the first thing that people notice and the last thing that they will remember about you. It is the most valuable part of your *Personal Brand*. This desire to be authentic is counter to the popular culture of our times; that is false, shallow and unsustainable. This **Mask Culture** is not positive and does not provide you with any vitalizing energy but seeks to take your energy and add it to its dysfunctional web of confusion.

Rejecting the Mask Culture is an action of *Self-Liberation* and requires the *Inner Wisdom* of your *Five Focal Facts* to guide you through all of its deceptive, irrelevant complexity.

The Mask Culture has constructed a world of unnecessary complexity that we are told is part of being a technologically sophisticated society.

*The truth is that Simplicity is the ultimate form of intellectual sophistication.*

With your liberated simplicity you also need to unplug from the destructive attributes of this dysfunctional complexity; **Distraction, Disruption** and **Distortion**. This trio destroys your sparkling energy and vitality. It is impossible to ever achieve the objectives of your Five Focal Facts if you allow this trio to dominate your mind and control your spirit.

You must be constantly vigilant to the influence the 3D's have upon you and construct a lifestyle culture that clears this clutter for your energy so that you can become the full potential of your essence; **Your Best Self.**

We are what we are Becoming. In that way if you desire to live the life of your Best Self you need to start today and live the future qualities that you seek to achieve. There will be of course peaks and valleys on the journey but three attributes define the most successful individuals I have worked with all these many years; being Brave, Bright and Bold.

The most important of all the three is being brave in the manner you passionately embrace the journey of your life and not being easily influenced away from your *Life Ethic and Guiding Logic.* I have had students of lesser intellectual aptitude whose brave determination has been the wind beneath their winged victory over their peers who were exceedingly more gifted. This courage has been their single most important success factor.

Strengthening that further is your compelling *True North Operating Philosophy* of **Simple Solutions, Smart Thinking** and **Strong Finish**. Living by this mantra dispels collective negative energy and demystifies the *Mask Culture's* graveyard of unnecessary complexity. It will preserve your energy and keep you on track.

*Discovering Your Truth* is the most important factor in defining the journey of your life. Unless this is accomplished it is impossible to successfully create your vision or establish any kind of legacy. Yet the choices are simple ones that are composed of thousands of automatic daily actions that just like breathing build strength to your **Inner Wisdom** with each passing positive behavior.

It ultimately becomes a matter of *Your Will* which is the truest expression of your essence and desire to live a quality positive life. Only a person who has faith in themselves can lead and have faith in others. This confidence is rooted in these solid and continuous lifestyle practices that collectively progress in a process of *Learning –Doing –Growing* Possessing this vital energy makes you shine like a star that attracts many into your bright positive orbits.

These orbits of influence with time become your creative, playful *Personal Culture.* This Personal Culture is the living legacy of your *Five Focal Facts.* Your Journey to Greatness has begun… For your have discovered your Inner Wisdom to become the master of your destiny.

# 2.

# Collective Intelligence

As MUCH AS WE HAVE BEEN TAUGHT BY OUR SOCIETY that the individual is the primary focus of all driving energies and achievements, from my experience, all positive successful individuals are always rooted in some form of **Community**.

The community affords and offers a wide range of nurturing energies that only improve the individual to further their ability to give, share and perfect their natural talents. In addition within the diversity of talents that the community offers, the individual will find no more optimal venue to learn and develop the talents that they do not naturally possess and must learn from other people.

The **Community of Purpose** is a dynamic and active environment where diverse individuals share a unity of intention; a single thread that unites and integrates many minds into a collective consciousness.

In our most fundamental design we were created to be social organisms who are not as the popular culture will have you believe, stand alone individual islands, but interactive, interdependent entities who *learn, achieve and grow* in a collective process of sharing, caring and loving each other. Humanity is *Tribal* by its nature as it affords so many supportively affirming elements beneficial to our growth.

In its purest form this *Community of Purpose* is a place that brings meaning to life and becomes the reference point to measure a wide rang of personal accomplishments and life achievements. Its nurturing energies are essential to possessing a healthy well-balanced mind and positive spirit.

It is impossible to find your truth or create your vision unless you are rooted in the learning experiences of a community. Your *Learning Legacy* reflects the cycle of birth, life and regeneration in which you pass your gift forward.

To understand this further one must have a functional knowledge of cognitive development; the natural intellectual process of how people learn, grow and develop. This is a beneficial point of reference when you are forming relationships as it will completely change the way your think about yourself and your relational intentions with other people.

In considering cognitive development there is first the things you do well. These are natural talents that you received the day you were born and are instinctively coded in your basic physiology; all you did was show up.

The only positive choice here is your *will* to use these skills wisely and perfecting them to the point that you become an expert in that specific area. Each individual is *accorded their own talent that is a unique gift* that, more than an option to be used wisely, it is their primary obligation in terms of their destiny to develop, share and polish them to a diamond like perfection.

The second cognitive element is *things you need to learn*, these are your *talent growth opportunities*. These list of talents did not come with the human package that was your designed model and received at birth. So to grow them you diligently need to work with patience and persistence. We are all so fortunate for within the *Community of Purpose* there is the collective intelligence and expertise to develop any talent you might like to improve.

It is up to you to find the correct resources and time to gain these new skills that will greatly enhance your selfhood and ability to develop the **Ultimate You**.

These two processes work well when there is an environment of mutual understanding as this is the firm foundation for all successful relationships. Relational interaction is best achieved within an environment of mutual caring and sharing where *Listening* is the primary focus of each interaction.

There is such a large amount of information to process and if your objective is to live a good quality life your task is to encourage vibrant dialogue as we learn twice as much when we are listening then when we are speaking.

It is best to view these diversity of talents as various personal expressions that creatively communicate the unique talents and *Personal Culture* that each one of us possess. These personal cultures are **Your Brand** that when well developed and managed expand your influence, impact and significance.

The key factor to remember is that your talent is only as useful as your ability to establish a relational environment that can create solutions and improve the quality of others peoples lives… Positive Life is not about being an armchair observer but a roll-up-your sleeves active participant.

Your **"I" Culture** is the manifestation of the attributes of your *Best Self*; for these behaviors express the objectives of your *Five Focal Facts*, your **Life Ethic, Guiding Logic** and **Compelling Passion**. Your "I" Culture serves as your *Vision Statement Platform* that is directed by your *Values and Virtues* as you seek to contribute your talents to the Community of Purpose. The "I" Culture's *Guiding Logic* is the engine that directs the manner you develop your relational standards.

*Inclusive, selfless, positive, hopeful, creative and innovative* in its character this "I" Culture becomes your trademark which builds your personal capital, esteem and significance in the Community of Purpose. This vision statement further develops to reflect your cumulative growth and eventually become the *Golden Legacy* of your life. All legacies find their life-creating source by making deposits into the community; not taking withdrawals as is the standard of the *Mask Culture*.

At the heart of the "I" Culture is your **Relationship Mindset** which is directed by answering a simple question. In your relational life; who wins? The answer to this reveals the manner you deal with everybody. If your mind is well balanced you desire everyone to win as when all the boats together rise higher in the tide; the greater good is served. When everyone wins your capital brand also continues to grow in its influence and wisdom; that's why win/win works so well for everyone.

If the answer is that you must always win, your short-sighted strategy will yield many temporary successes but is not sustainable as your capital is reduced with each selfish transaction. Successful individuals build their capital in a community context.

Time remains the single most important factor to a positive, quality life. Successful individuals strive to do everything correctly the first time. Duplicated effort is an unproductive use of time and energy. Having a **Unifying Philosophy** about the manner you approach all of your tasks, create solutions and then effectively execute their results significantly benefits the quality of your life. This completely destroys the impact of *Distraction, Disruption* and *Distortion* in your day-to-day existence and produces a healthy sense of *Clarity, Precision* and *Urgency.*

The simple philosophy of directing your life to be **On Task, On Point, On Time** establishes the quality standard of excellence that your "I" Culture seeks to achieve. It further becomes yet another definer of *Your Brand* as it further enhances your skill sets, capital value but more significantly your influence leadership.

Now that you have built your thought platform and equipped it with a wide range of tools in your toolbox, it is time to further impact your environment by advancing your *"I" Culture into the community space.* In your journey you will meet like minded souls who share your collective positive vision. From this emerges a **"We" Culture** who recognize the diversity of talent and opportunity for mutual growth in the community context.

This *Collective Culture* is founded with like minds that may share many of your perceptions but not all of them. Yet its core unifying philosophy is one of *mutual respect, dialogue, support, cooperation and learning* that it consistently seeks to represent. The **"We" Culture** imparts a host of vitalizing energies to the individuals and provides a vehicle to create a stable, positive quality of life in the nurturing context of the entire community.

The Collective Culture is also a counter balance to the dysfunction of the exclusive, elite **"Us" Culture** whose *self-oriented, self-interested objectives* undermine the values and virtues of the Community of Purpose. It is this "US" Culture that must be vigorously exposed in the falsehood of their beliefs and their desire to *limit the opportunity of all members of the community.*

How does one rise above the elite and powerful whose resources are limitless? First, by not playing their game, by establishing your own standards and by living a good quality life with your own rules. Life is not a contest of who possessed the most material things but a journey in which whose footprint and contribution will remain long after they are gone. Creativity is far more valuable than wealth.

In this *Vision Quest of Selfhood* we must all be very brave and assert our **Champion Leadership** which is bright and bold. This *Champion Culture* creates an environment of opportunity for its community, changes lives and leaves an endearing legacy that helps guide generations to come.

This Collective Intelligence requires *Simple Solutions, Smart Thinking* and the ability to sustain the long journey and have a *Strong Finish.* It ultimately all rests on *Your Will* and the nurturing energies you provide yourself and that you obtain from others in your *Golden Circle of Trust.*

*Your Champion Leadership understands that its positive energy can prevail over any obstacle.* This *Can-Do Attitude* is forged in the hot fires of many personal struggles. The hotter these fires, the better the steel they produce and the more resilient you are to sustain the journey and to win many victories that you will accomplish. These victories are not single-minded achievements but are collective experiences that bond you even closer to your Community of Purpose.

Your *Collective Intelligence* and *Inner Wisdom* find their truth in centering your mind within the energies of archetypal principles that will serve you well every day of your life. Your positive energy is founded on truth and a compelling desire to possess the *Correct View, Correct Intention* and follow through with the *Correct Action.*

You can only have the Correct View if you are a **Right Being** and believe that you are the responsible *Consciousness of all your Decisions.* It is a statement of your will and final determination that creates your quality life. The Correct Intention comes in being **Right Knowing** in which your take total accountability as the *Enabler of the Task.* It is your Simple Solutions and Smart Thinking that gets and keeps everything going in the right direction.

Correct Action is attempting to be **Right Doing** as the *Facilitator of the Process* that gives their all and their best every time and in that selfless effort achieves a victory even before the objective has been won.

While many will choose to be a bright leaf blown be the winds of change, listen to your strength, find your centered humility; become the change that you seek to find. Root yourself in the *Collective Intelligence* and energies of the Community of Purpose. Focus your thinking on always trying to help and work with other people to create the win/win victories.

Declare your Self-Liberation from the distractions of the confusing "US' Culture. *No longer be tossed by the waves of change but evolve and become the creative energy that creates and moves the waves forward.*

The Power of Positive You is actuated on the path of Discovering Your Truth.

# 3.

# Positive Perception

THE ABILITY TO MASTER THE ART OF PERCEPTION is essential if you desire to positively influence the world around you. A strong mastery of perception is found in possessing a deeper understanding of the energies of your selfhood.

This *Synergy of Self* is the distinct combination of energies that reveal your unique footprint. Our *Total Self* is a dynamic reaction of many stimuli that are constantly competing to become the predominate energy in your personal world.

There are two processes that direct the flow of thoughts, feelings and behaviors. They find their source in basic genetic coding of our DNA. They are instinctive energies that helped the human species to not only survive but to evolve and thrive as the predominate life form on the planet.

Our intuition and perception are the most obvious manifestation of these energies working within us. Due to this, intuitive thought is far more effective and predictive than rational thought. In mastering the Art of Perception one must become more finely tuned with their intuitional dimensions; the powerful energies of our unconsciousness. Our intuition is ceaselessly working to align our energies as to optimize their impact. It is an isometric process that is active, volatile and expansive. **Active Balance** seeks to combine our energies in a manner to optimize the *natural talents of our selfhood*. There is a defined if not predictable rhythm to its constant motion. Working with its intuitive rhythm produces a more perfected expertise of our natural talents.

**Creative Tension** is volatilely expansive as it pushes and prods our Will to improve, develop and grow. It is a spark that fires constantly and the key element is to learn how to manage it. To ignore it, we risk living a static and unfulfilled life. To agitate it, we create a flame too hot that is not sustainably healthy. The moderation of this spark is found in your ability to master the tempo of the Creative Tension dynamic. I am reminded of the moth flying around the bright, hot candle…. Too far- not enough heated light…Too Close- total destruction.

Our life's journey is a long one and the effective use of our energies is one of the great challenges of our existence .. *Slow and Steady Always Wins the Race.*

All of us are empowered with four basic energies that we must utilize each one in a proportional amount on a daily basis if we desire to optimize our strength and vigor. *Intellectual, Emotional, Physical and Spiritual* energies create this *Synergy of Self.* The wise use of each of these in accordance with *Active Balance and Creative Tension* provides remarkable total health and sustained vitality that only improves with age as we learn through our cumulative experiences to master them more completely.

There is no fixed recipe here. It is all a matter of blocking out the toxic *"Us' Culture,* listening to your intuition to learning the rhythm of your *Total Self.* In mastering the many dimensions of all these forces you will have established the foundation for understanding the value and purpose of *360 Perception.*

Positive Perception is not some shallow marketing strategy to promote your personal brand but an functional knowledge of what works for you and how you have to flex and modify yourself so you can successfully engage with all types of people.

*Relational Development* is best understood by the chemistry of engagement that we encounter each time we meet a new individual. Each new individual is an entire new universe in your life and opportunity for you to grow.

**Self-Identification** is our **Interior View** and how we communicate with other people. This is our *Self Image* which does possess some level of importance in our ability to be resilient and persevere through adversity but in terms of our ability to effectively communicate it is a very misleading indicator.

The true measure of our effectiveness is the **Exterior View**. This is how other people view your image, hear your message and form a **Mutual Association** with you. This is the formational space where all relationships find a bonding attraction or do not have that certain " Click" and reciprocity to create anything.

This ability to observe, *listen, inquire, engage, inform, educate and inspire* is yet another complex relationship dance that is completely unique to each person who you encounter. To empower the influence of *Positive You* there must be one central premise that you passionately follow... *Nothing is ever about You and Everything That You Do is about Everybody Else.* This simple and humble statement will change your life and completely change the way you interact and come to appreciate the many talented and helpful people that surround you every day. Remember, the giver receives much more in benefit than the recipient.

This ability to step outside of yourself to constantly objectify your behaviors impact on other people and the goals that you seek to achieve is extremely valuable for it opens your eyes to many new possibilities in your life. This is not an easy task as it requires a determination to re-wire your impulses, feelings and thoughts from the traditional manner that have let your unconscious run your life.

This enhanced Self Awareness is an amazing liberating experience.

Part of your Self-Liberation is to take control of these run-away energies to develop strategies that are designed to not just work when all is calm but especially in those stressful moments. This is where your new enhanced Self-Awareness kicks-in and after a series of personal victories, the satisfaction you will receive will make it impossible for you to go back to doing things the way you used to.

The recognition of these skills are the beginning of jump-starting your **Toolbox Technology**. This *Portable Wisdom* is your 24/7 companion where ever you are and becomes a most powerful intellectual and emotional support. The more you use these tools, the more you learn to ebb and flow with their rhythm until they will become second nature with your thoughtful actions.

With this mastery there develops an amazing *Synergy, Synchronicity and Synthesis* of your energies that are fine-tuned like an engine of a race car that works with dynamic precision to produce remarkable clarity and focus on a multilevel basis.

What makes it even more impactful is the *Mindfulness* that you bring to each new relationship. You live the good life of *Your Best Self* and with clarity execute behaviors and strategies to produce excellence not only for you but for an ever widening circle of other individuals who witness your leadership abilities.

This *Learning Leadership* is the natural extension of your selfhood and the valued contribution *Your Best Self* has given to the Community of Purpose.

Within the context of your "We" Culture all *Learning Leaders* gather a group of diverse individuals to help center and objectify their perception. This group of nurturing relationships are essential to keep you focused and directed with the *Correct View, Correct Intention and Correct Actions*.

All *Learning Leaders* know that we are social creations that were designed to listen, develop and grow together; sustainable knowledge is collaborative by its nature.

The more multigenerational and diverse this group is in terms of their experiences, the more valuable their information is as they provide you a more complete 360 *Perspective*. Your *Wisdom Team* is a dynamic group of relationships who become a most vital part of your life and increasingly more esteemed as the years pass. To keep it vitally vibrant you must selectively continue to bring new energy into your *Circle of Trust*; for this is the cycle of live and regeneration.

This circle of trusted advisors are *Investment Relationships* that are the most significant and valuable assets in your life. These are not the *"Drive-Through"* relationships of the "Us" Culture but authentic nurturing relationships that may have their relational spikes and dips but are life-long vital energies that only leave you when they pass away. Yet even in their passing; the wisdom they have imparted into you remains forever as it is a spiritual energy and not effected by time and space.

What makes this Wisdom Team dynamic is the wealth of talents that it provides access to you; a mutual exchange of the *Things You Do Well* and the *Things You Need To Learn*. It is a personal space that further exercises the energies of your *Active Balance and Creative Tension*. For an individual who is interested in self-improvement, empowerment and transformation your Wisdom Team is your right hand.

Living a positive good quality life requires a determination to pursue a *Vision Quest* in order to not only discover your truth but to authenticate specifically this truth to who you are and what you desire to become. There can be no authentic vision or ability to truly understand the mystery of relationships and their many benefits unless the individual takes the time to experience this introspective journey.

We clearly make a choice either to master our selfhood or to find various forms of distractions and excuses to run away from its live-creating *Inner Wisdom*.

We were designed to be a dynamic, every changing creation guided by our *Inner Wisdom*. That is our destiny and nothing less than its complete fulfillment is a limited life journey of diminished quality. It is never too late to change the circumstances of your life. Be it great or small changes, every one that brings joy and fulfillment to you is a most positive step that you should celebrate with your victorious spirit that bravely prevails over all impediments…this is hard work!

Discovering Your Truth is the gateway and starting point of Creating Your Vision.

# Part II

# Creating Your Vision

# 4.

# Wisdom Team

CRAFTING A LONG-TERM, COMMITTED VISION is one of the most excitingly enjoyable parts of our life. *The person who makes their work- their play never works a single day*. Here is where your *Compelling Passion* becomes your daily compass that through your intuitive perception directs the building of your *Personal Vision*.

No one created a vision and successfully executed it all by themselves but in the context of a **Community of Purpose**. This requires a network of diverse people who bring the wealth of their talent resources to support you.

Having an understanding of relationships and various forms of relational energy will greatly enhance the successful execution of your vision. Becoming a *Personality Expert* is a critical factor in developing the level of discernment necessary to build all of the teams, groups and organizations that will surround you all of your life.

*Human Capital* is the most valuable of all performing assets and the management of its energies is an art form of skillful sincerity.

The creative combination of these personalities actually accelerate your effectiveness as it empowers a unique dynamic chemistry that make you a *Stand-Out Brand* in a world that is filled with so much mediocrity.

Sustainable excellence can be achieved by always focusing on the quality of the relationships in your many circles. To neglect or ignore this consideration is a fatal flaw that will impair if not derail your ability to expand your Personal Vision.

From my experience of being a part of so many wonderful efforts there are four distinct **Talent Mindsets** that are easily identified through the manner they deal with challenges and apply their specific **Solution Strategy**.

These Solution Strategies reveal in an instant the way they think. This thinking is an automatic *stimulus-response* that is rooted in their DNA. It is as personal as a finger print and is the talent that they do best, easily and with precise near effortless accuracy; for it is the unique gift you received at birth.

These four Talent Mindsets are driven by two different types of energy. Intellectual energy fuels the **Analytical** and **Deductive** minds. Emotional energy inspires the **Creative** and **Empathic** intentions.

**ACHIEVERS** apply the *Analytical* method to their **Solution Strategy** in which they divide the challenge into many small parts, reorganizes the dots and reconnect them in a new more productive configuration.

**INVESTIGATORS** apply the *Deductive* method and meticulously research the root cause, verify its validity and justify the course of action upon a very specific set of standards.

**CONTRIBUTORS** infer and infuse their *Creative Imagination* to the challenge at hand, think out of the box and communicate several unique solution strategies to get the task accomplished.

**COMMUNICATORS** elicit their *Empathic* beliefs of cooperative collaboration as the best solution strategy. The collective efforts of the *Community of Purpose* possesses mutual consensus that is superior to any other approach; as it is the one with the greatest possibility for sustained results.

To add another layer of expertise to be considered.

Each mindset has a very specific influencing style and primary motivation.

Achievers **Empower** with the objective of building **Confidence** to maximize the talents of those who surround them.

Investigators **Validate** with their precise observations to build **Trust** in establishing a level of authentic interaction.

Contributors **Inspire** with their gifted and colorful imaginations to allow an open and **Creative** environment.

Communicators **Embrace** our shared values and smooth the rough edges of the debate to consider the superior results that **Collaboration** achieves.

# Analytical Achievers

The Achiever is the great Coordinator of Resources, Projects and all Initiatives. This Talent Mindset is highly motivated. They are usually the Tallest Blade of Grass in every organization and possess a vital energy that sparkles and makes them extremely attractive.

## TALENT

- Charismatic Dynamic Persona

- Decisive Determined Confidence

- Intensely Focused Intellect

- Strategic Organized Execution

- Consistent Productive Achievement

## GROWTH

- Impulsive Impatient Tendencies

- Impaired Listening & Deliberative Skills

- Hyperactive Overbearing Engagement

- Over-Confident Assumptions

• Inflexible Dominating Judgement

# Deductive Investigators

The Investigator's highly engaged deductive mind is constantly processing information which is always measured against some set of standards. The Rule of Law governs this persona who is an uncompromising Advocate for Quality and Sustaining a Standard of Excellence in everything they do.

## TALENT

• Disciplined Logical Intellect

• Detailed Precise Execution

• Mindful Meticulous Analysis

• Intensive Exhaustive Investigation

• Dynamic Principled Leadership

## GROWTH

• Inflexible Extreme Stubbornness

• Rigid Uncreative Imagination

• Limited Listening & Engagement Skills

• Unsupportive Determined Opposition

• Obsessive Compulsive Perfection

# Creative Contributors

The Contributor is like the early morning with the Sun Always Rising. Their infectious energy is essential to any organization that desires growth and future development. They are the Visionary of New Opportunities with their unbridled and sincere optimism.

## TALENT

• Original Unique Creativity

• Intuitive Instant Perception

• Sensitive Responsive Empathy

• Ingenious Innovative Imagination

• Passionate Enthusiastic Engagement

## GROWTH

• Overly Theoretical and not Practical

• Zealously Inclusive without Critical Judgement

• Disinterested with In-Depth Investigative Analysis

• Unrealistic Expectations

• Needs Approval and Affirmation

# Empathetic Communicators

The Communicator serves the most critical role in so many organizations; a Bridge that Joins Everyone Together. Their cooperative spirit makes them the center of trust and this is why they are an Expert on Managing Human Capital.

## TALENT
- Caring Supportive Intentions
- Superior Listening & Responsive Skills
- Authentic Loyal Collaboration
- Cooperative Flexible Partnership
- Dependable Trusted Consistency

## GROWTH
- Strong Need For Validation
- Idealistic Intention without Discernment
- Impulsive Enthusiasm Absent Analysis
- Emotionally Driven & Overly Sensitive
- Passive Aggressive Engagement Style

I further refined my **Wisdom Team Types** by their **Talent-** *Things They Do Well* and their **Growth-** *Things They Need To Learn*. When I am attempting to objectify my opinion on something that is important, these *Talent Types* instantly direct my *compass* to the best expertise and assist me in not wasting time on things that do not work. We all have circles of experts who surround us and the secret is knowing how to effectively work with them in the collaborative process to acquire their skills.

There also emerges from these *Talent Types* a specific *Team Leadership Role* that each *Talent Mindset* is absolutely superior in performing. I have tested and re-tested this concept to establish its valid correlation to produce consistent results. These Team Leadership Roles are a *True North* as their mindsets create a defined *Solution Strategy*; for each strategy has an appropriate success factor to the type of challenge.

In bringing together any organization it is necessary to have a balanced blend of all four **Talent Types** as it adds many dimensions to your efforts. Each of these diverse talents all possess uniquely crafted energies that when brought together produce consistently superior results each and every time due to the chemistry their collectivism creates.

There must be a healthy respect for the gifts that each *Talent Type* contributes for all are equal in the *Community of Purpose*. Just because certain *Talent Types* manifest a more directive role or tone does not confer them with any more priority or intrinsic value over the other typologies. Many organizations get caught in this trap and it is to their detriment as it builds a one-sided *"Us" Culture* that possesses a pervasive inequality that impairs the creative blending of all *Talent Types*. This culture limits the opportunity for everyone to participate and bring their unique Solution Strategy.

These long-term *Investment Relationships* possess a rich quality that makes for enjoyable surroundings with happy people that *never work a single day; for their work is their passionate play*. These type of environments spark innovative growth as they allow people to stretch themselves to new levels of excellence because they feel strongly supported.

Learning to observe, listen and evaluate these *Talent Types* will greatly enhance your perception. Educating yourself to know the *growth-edge* that each Talent Type struggles with provides further insightful opportunity for you to develop your *Learning Leadership*. Investment Relationships are all about leading everyone forward together.

In that *Learning Leadership* your skill is working successfully with all four Talent Mindsets which creates an opportunity to increase your *Personal Culture's influence*. Mastering the learning technology of human capital is a life-long pursuit of your positive engagement…one that few people actual ever truly perfect.

# 5.

# Investment Relationships

HERE IS WHERE THE RUBBER REALLY HITS THE ROAD and all this theoretical waxing you express needs to be backed-up by real life behaviors and positive actions.

The efficient use of your energy is challenged and tested by how you construct the many orbits that emanate from your *Learning Leadership*. This *Personal Culture* which is as unique as your fingerprint becomes your brand. It is what people remember about you and what they say about you when you are not in their presence. Its external authenticity manifests the internal reality of your *Inner Life*. What we think about is where we live and where we live is the source of our optimal, centered selfhood.

Within the many dimensions of your mind, in the privacy of its actions here is where the core of the nuclear reactor splits the atoms of feelings and thoughts into a stew of chemicals that engages, channels, empowers, transforms and finally transcends the essence of who they are, what they will become and what will remain after they are gone. This cosmic perspective illuminates **Archetypal Energies** that directs your unconsciousness to be the engine driving both your intuition and perception. Our unconsciousness is a vast mysterious iceberg; mostly unseen but very influential.

This hyper -intensive space is inspired by your spiritual energies or motivated by your humanistic philosophies. It is a place of unquenchable, unconditional love. When this kicks-into gear, people truly sparkle and their outward physical manifestations only further confirms their inner workings are buzzing along. This vitalizing energy I most awkwardly have come to call *Karma* as its fluid, elusive energy is so hard to describe.

It is a life force energy that you feel when you are with certain people. To the spiritual believers we would witness " God is with Us." To a more secular mind it evokes a well integrated individual of *Values and Virtues*. Yet to both types of thinking, this is an individual that you want to spend time with and have as a big part of your life.

Such people are a real gift and fill our days of much work and concerns with a bright spark that makes everything so much easier to do. The thing that I find fascinating about this type of positive person; *they are always doing something good for somebody else*. The process of giving and doing actually continues to strengthen these people both intellectually and emotionally for a lifetime.

Their *Good Karma* actually comes to benefit them more than anyone else for they are remarkably healthy people. Their vitality secret is the healthy workings of their mind!

*The emptying of self is the perfection of self.* People that do lots of good works come to develop an amazingly healthy lifestyle and mental outlook that only continues to improves with experience. They also have the ability to step outside themselves and reflect upon their behavior. This perspective makes it easy for them to laugh at themselves and possess a level of self-appraisal that is instructively insightful.

This *Mindfulness* is authentically powerful. In our world of so many temporary, fake if not socially toxic individuals this mindful energy is always quickly noticed; for it is just so appealing. People may not know how to rationally explain or describe it but their instinctive intuition absorbs this energy and likes what it feels. This wholeness possesses a certain integrity that has a clean, bubbly quality that kind of reminds me of the efflorescence of a sparkling glass of champagne.

So many people live in the *"Us" Culture* and drink its waters. The more they drink this water, the more thirsty they become until their confusion makes them believe that this is how life is supposed to be lived. There is the false external flash but not the real efflorescent sparkle. To anyone who lives in the circles of *Inner Wisdom* their absence of integrity is known at first impression as our intuition rejects their falsehood.

It is impossible to develop *Investment Relationships* when you live a life of **Escapism** and believe that you are unaccountable to anyone. It is hard to do the diligent work of cooperative consensus when you live a life of **Entitlement**. It is difficult to respectfully love your neighbor when **Incivility's** judgements rule your days and nights. When **Materialism** and **Greed** direct every goal you seek to achieve then all people are just temporary moments who are only as useful as what they can do for you. These are the fruits of the *"Us" Culture's* bitter harvest who also advocate the falsehood of *youth and beauty over the wisdom of age and experience.*

The positive person daily rejects these philosophies and insures that their influences have as little as possible inner impact in their life. I am not advocating any type of monastic life for that is to reject the world. What is far better, is to live in the very midst of all this nonsense having the *Inner Wisdom* to smile and just say NO. This is the leadership platform for the *Brave, Bright and the Bold* who love the smell of fresh air and freedom.

They have declared their **Self-Liberation** ..there is no other feeling quite like it!

Once you have these sweet fruits it is impossible to return to this confused darkness. Fortunate are the *Children of the Light* who take pride in their rejection of the popular culture and earnestly seek to convert many to their *Inner Wisdom*.

The *Positive You* does not passively shrink from confronting the toxic culture. Actually quite the opposite is true. Positive You is a *Learning Leader* who directs the optimistic values of the Community of Purpose. It is from this mutual platform that your leadership and its orbits of influence exponentially expand.

**"We" Culture** advances the principle of *Trust, Learning, Cooperation, Achievement and Innovation.* These are the frameworks of your thoughtful response to the social illness of the "Us" Culture. These attributes are the counter balance to *Escapism, Entitlement, Materialism, Incivility and Greed.* The "We" Culture's values and virtues are tools in your toolbox that will empower your ascent.

Mindful of this, your behavior fills your world with a core of individuals who support your *Inner Wisdom* belief structure. Your *Wisdom Team* become a strong compass who help preserve your direction. These are not walls of warriors, like an army to fight an adversary but circles of positive energy's unconditional love that lift you up far above all the nonsense so that you come to a place where all of the noisy clutter of the "US" Culture has nothing to do with the way you live. Like a person who awoke from a long sleep you see the world with newly bright eyes holding deep inside you a secret wise strength that makes you always safe.

From this vantage point you can deal with the most toxic and totally impudent people with astounding kindness but also with a clear directness that completely confounds them; for you are able to accomplished any thing, anywhere with anybody.

Through many years of experience comes the ability to perfect this *Inner Wisdom.* Your consistent execution of your authenticated wisdom makes you a *Thought* and **Influence Leader** whose reputation for successful solution strategies proceed you.

*Champion Leaders create only future leaders and never followers.*

Your role in this leadership position is to *inform, educate, encourage and inspire* anyone who is part of your daily life. With this *Collective Trust* there comes much *responsibility* to be a role model of sincere integrity. Your ethical core is central to your leadership authenticity and sets you apart from the values of the "Us" Culture. It was easily explained to me, *once you know who you are and do not want to be anyone but yourself* you acquire a certain leadership attractiveness.

I surmise there can be nothing more *authentic* than having an integrated, positive *self-image* that is also both quietly confident, caring and humble; no wonder it possesses such an attractiveness.

Your enhanced selfhood along with the tools in your toolbox that have created a record of achievement have prepared you to step up to an opportunity that is most challengingly rewarding. A transformational experience that I have come to call **Your Ultimate Inspiration**. It is about desiring to be the best, giving your best and expecting always for the best outcomes. The mastery of your *Active Balance* and *Creative Tension* will be the rocket fuel that launches the *Ultimate You*.

We live daily with so much mediocrity and have become desensitized to how it is slowly deteriorating the quality of our life. This the deception of the elitely exclusive "US" Culture who seeks total control to further advance their self interest at the expense of the Community of Purpose. Theirs is an untraditional approach as the achievements of the successful American Century tell us a much different story of inclusion, equality and populism.

*If your expect only the very best that is exactly what you are going to get!* So **Positive You** is an optimist who sees every glass more than half full and every person with a gift to be shared with the entire world. This *Personal Culture* and lifestyle philosophy day-by-day builds your *Ultimate You House of Wisdom*.

It is of primary importance to become a *Personality Expert and Human Capital Technician* able to dissect the many layers of relational exchange. In the complexity of these exchanges and your ability to re-architect these experiences you will find quantum growth in the many circles of the people within your *House of Wisdom*. These skills become a key part of your *Ultimate You Brand* that with time builds your influence in the Community of Purpose.

This *Ultimate You Brand* is a state of mindfulness that fuels the *Investment Relationship Dynamic*. These relationships are long-term and in some cases lifelong mutual engagements where everyone learns and grows together. This is not some abstract theory but something that I have witnessed in its real-life success. The *Circle of Trust* is the starting point where you are the center lynchpin coordinating a culture of positive thoughts, feelings and behaviors.

This *Relationship Mindset* is one that wants everyone to win. Your *Circle of*

*Trust* accepts the learning premise of **Talent-** *Things You Do Well* and **Growth-** *Things You Need To Learn* as a guiding working knowledge framework of how each person possesses a predominate *Talent Mindset.* These frameworks establish the boundaries of the *Investment Relationship Dynamic.*

This dynamic process is like my favorite professional web site in which I have over one thousand connections in twenty six countries who are a part of my collective, personal, global universe. This web site conveys the diversity of talents and the endless combinations of mutual exchange experiences that are possible.

This web site is my *Mutual Communications Platform*; the foundation of my *Learning Leadership.* I am consistently amazed how effective this website is in co-ordinating all my global relationships in a very user friendly manner.

While this does a great job, nothing can replace one-to-one in person dialogue. Here is where you will sharpen your skills in becoming a *Personality Expert and Human Capital Technician.* Developing this takes patience, experiential practice and a keen self-awareness to the many intricacies of our five senses. *Acute Listening, Insightful Observation, Intuitive Rapid Analysis* not debilitated by excess rational thought are the perceptive skill that need to be perfected.

There are no cookie cutter recipes here. Mastering this requires *Emotional Self-Regulation*, disciplined precision, a refined diligence to every small detail and a multi-generational knowledge how people of various ages mutually interact.

My process attempts to break into bite-size pieces the art form of human relational exchange. It is not the ultimate and only process but it is one that works well for me. I have attempted to simplify this process which is by its nature a spontaneous, perceptive and intuitive mix that is difficult to quantify. So much of this process's interplay is the energy of that large unconscious iceberg that is not completely seen but runs the show. My process frameworks are only as useful in how they direct you in a learning process until you can do these things with the much more proficient automatic *unconscious Reaction- Response mechanism.*

Applying the **360 Perception** theory of how we *see ourselves and how other people see us* is a useful point of reference in the majority of social situations. It is also a great competitive advantage as the vast majority of people do not have any self-awareness of these relational dynamics. Each personal interaction has the potential of being a learning moment; an opportunity to improve the quality of the relationship with the person you are engaging…. this is a key point to remember.

The *Investment Relationship* process seeks to empower your entire network with the benefits of your Positive Personal Culture and to maximize every opportunity moment. Once you absorb the energy of the process it becomes a natural part of who you are and what you do. *The laboring oar is finding out which process works for you and is authenticated to your relationship style.*

# I.   Energy Exchange

**Investment Relations** are all about developing an environment that is mutual in which your mindset is keenly focused on studying human behavior. In addition you need to rely strongly on your intuitive and perceptive skills to direct the process. These unconscious energies will direct the natural flow that will become a rhythm and method of how you engage people. The success factor here is to do every thing in this process instinctively. It takes some time to master this but when you authenticate which process works for you; the effectiveness of your abilities will surprise you.

## TRANSLATE

This is a mind-shift for many people who are always speaking…Stop.. Be Silent!

With the knowledge of the four **Talent Mindsets,** Look, Listen, Absorb and feel the energy, use of words, visual and body cues to develop a *ten second analysis.*

How do they Act? What are they doing? Now the most important question is, why and for what motivation to achieve which objective? What is not said but is observed? Think of your task here like translating a foreign language into a format you can both quickly understand and form some mutual association.. the exchange has begun.

## TRANSCEND

This is a little more difficult but essential to the process. With the information you have gathered and your knowledge of the four Talents Mindsets, you need to step right into the other person's shoes. Here is where you develop your best skills as a personality expert. This is part of the investment process as you seek to deepen your knowledge of the other person and begin to understand which path of communication works best for them. What is their interactional style?

## TEACH

Now it is the time to offer support and personalize your advice as it removes so much judgment from the process and makes for a much less threatening environment. Be extremely specific in your examples and reference them with many real-life situations. Use this to objectify your observations or opinions as it demonstrates sincerity and the strength of your authenticity… this is your **Learning Leadership** at its best moment.

# II.  Magic Moment

This is the opportunity moment where the lost art of excellent discussion needs to find a new level of open engagement. Here is an arena where great ideas, strengths, talents and many mutual learning moments take place. What makes it magic is when there is sincere mutual exchange which is an unselfish sharing of two people who are mutually depositing their talent and knowledge into each other. Such a rare giving of self does happen and for **Positive You** it is the keystone of who you are and what you do.

## COMMUNICATE

Some people get confused and believe that communications is all about speaking but actually effective communicators are acute listeners. Our mind learns twice as much when we are listening then speaking. The art form here is the core of **360 Perception,** to not only have a personal level of understanding but to have the perception to know that your message is understood in its clarity by the other person. You must always be mindful of the strengths and challenges each **Talent Mindset** possess and seek to tailor your method to use their strengths and assist them with their challenges.

Good discussion is a **Dialogue** not a **Monologue** by one dominate party. If you find that you are the one always speaking then just stop because you are not totally conveying your message. You must use your emotional self more to gage this dynamic than your intellectual self. The objective here is to set the stage for creating solutions in which the strengths of the diversity of Talent Mindsets can excel.

## CONFIGURE

This is where the information, like a raw product is processed into the beginning of the final product, in which the unique Solution Strategies of Directors, Judges, Philosophers and Facilitators present options, opinions and opportunities that demonstrate their individual strengths. The discussion is enriched by having the background knowledge of the four Talent Mindsets and valuing the expertise of each participant.

When done well Configuring is an experiential laboratory that is charged with creative energies that form an Innovation Platform where no concept is left unconsidered. This is the Ultimate You Magic Moment an opportunity to bring other people closer and more mutually joined in your influence orbits. This is the laser laboratory where clarity and precision creates world class thinking and creative ingenuity.

# III. Big Bang

As the name implies, here is where the greatest learning moments of the Investment Relationship process takes place. Along with the lost art form of dialogue comes the even more challenging environment of compromise and consensus. So much positive and creative energy is wasted through people's inability to find common ground. Hopefully in possessing a more intensive knowledge of each individual's personality, natural talents but more importantly their under-developed abilities an entirely more productive method of finalizing a *collective solution mindset can emerge.*

## CONVERGE

A creative mixture of your Thinking and Feeling Self is in order to map out a process that allows the best solutions to rise to the top. Convergence is all about **Blending & Bending** ideas, opinions and options. It is a messy affair and requires maturity and a great deal of **Emotional Self-Regulation**. There is no cookie cutter method to do this but having some framework and collectively agreeing to specific boundaries sure does make the process more efficient. Personal agendas and factions only still further muddy the waters and ensure that the solution chosen has very little effective sustainability.

My own approach is to list the available solution options and give each points for merit but conversely subtract points for their weakness. It does not take long through this objective process for the best strategy to rise to the top as the win/ win solution.

## CONSENSUS

If all the parts of the process are well executed creating a compromise of opinions to achieve a consensus easily comes together. My method is to think of all the participants and information as the **Pieces**. The challenge and complexity of the solution is the **Puzzle**. The collective set of Solution Strategies I engage is my **Process**. The consensus is the final **Product** which is the sum total of the Pieces, Puzzle and the Process.

The other key factor is having a mindset that thinks of everything as a part of a long-term strategy. This is the **Wisdom Team Philosophy** who rejects all short term transactions but seeks long-term relationship experiences that mutually invest in each other's future.

*Learning and Growing is a Team Sport.. No one becomes successful all by themselves.*

# Part III

# Establishing Your Legacy

# 6.

# Positivity

OUR LIFE... A FANTASTIC JOURNEY OF SELF-DISCOVERY that drop by drop collects into a vast personal reservoir of Self-Knowledge. The challenge is all the choices we must daily make that in their cumulative impact year after year form into the solidified image of who we are. A terrifying thought to some people while to other people an absolutely delicious adventure. It all comes down to such simple choices of how you want to look at the world and conceive your place within it.

The single most important aspect of being a positive, light filled person is an abundance of gratitude in your heart. It pulses through the veins in your body, it brightens every thought to compel your kind compassion and makes you so incredibly happy the vast majority of every day you live. *Your good thoughtful actions are the best companions in this life.* They are my best friends for they are always a part of all my adventurous journeys. I am never alone but always in their company of comfortable warmth that never let's me down; for they consistently serve me so well.

This wellspring of **Invincible Optimism** stares down debilitating depression, creatively problem solves with ease the most complex, stressful situations while it adds vitality to mollify and detoxify the pathological pressures of twenty first century life. This optimism's greatest contribution is its perspective of wise discernment that changes lives. This discernment compels you to unconditionally accept people to come together an accomplish wondrous things. It is virtual sunshine in a bottle that all you have to do is open the top and its magic does its thing every time.

With this abundant gratitude in your heart, *Entitlement, Escapism, Materialism, Incivility and Greed* find no place to take root. They are foreign concepts that are temporary low energy behaviors that you find shallow if not completely boring. More than some level of moral outrage, repugnancy and judgement of their harmful nature you simply turn away from these ridiculous behaviors; for they quite simply have nothing to do with your life.

I want to be where the sun is always rising, a place where its shines every day for this is the destination that the Divine One designed for me; a place of unquenchable love that is created by someone who loves me more. It is the spirits of my ancestors who made a choice to embrace the Divine One, walk in His ways and celebrate life each and every day. The spirit of the Divine One and my beloved ancestors empower my positive energy as I embody their earthly spirit; continuing their tradition of care.

Not that my vision needs to be yours but you must live with a vision in your heart. What is your image of Nirvana? If you do not have a personal Nirvana as a part of your daily life, no wonder you are not positively joyful. We are not human creations living a spiritual life but spiritual creations living a human life. The *Spirit* and your own personal definition of what that is and what that provides to you is your core of strength.

There are so many things in life that are unexplainable and little miracles happen every day. Are they coincidence or are they just the *Spirit* being discreet? I daily without hesitation call upon the *Spirit* to come and assist whoever is with me in a wide variety of tasks. Call me Pollyanna but it always comes; getting the job done well.

The *Spirit* is the power generator that lights all your light bulbs and without it your existence is vastly diminished. If you are lost and searching to find yourself you need go no further than into your interior self for that is where your Spirit resides. Disconnect from the toxic noisy nonsense of our present world and put it on hold for a while. Push through the cobwebs of the unused places in your mind to re-light the lampstands that are always there to bring you their bright wisdom. Pony-up and take on your psychic demons, those dysfunctional constellations that the "US" Culture has brought to pollute your *Spirit*, dampen your will power and halt your growth.

Visualize your battle with these negative energies. Be fierce in your opposition to them as they will not go away easily. They will morph into a host of different appealing thoughts and feelings to confuse your rational mind and weaken your will-power. Be vigilant as they are a determined adversary who know you very well. Be persistent in your opposition as you may struggle but you will beat them.

What emerges in your liberating victory is an awakening epiphany of self that does not happen over night but it comes when you least suspect it. It is quite startling as I have witnessed this with my students many times. A new awakening brightness suddenly appearing in their eyes. Yet it does not remain permanent unless there has been a transformation in their lifestyle. I suspect that this brightness is a reflection of awakened *Active Balance* in their minds; for their spirit has found its nurturing source in a safe place of strength and peace... what a gift!

This exercise is much more difficult for the people who love the materialism and status of this world for they must reject so much of the attributes of their own self image and sadly admit they wasted their time following such false gods. How hard it must be to look in the mirror and not like what you see... change comes through accepting the truth and a strong belief that in redemption we find new strength.

No one can possess the orbits of *Positivity* unless they first have emerged victorious over their negative energies and then invested themselves in developing their *Inner Life* to a state of optimal health. The bravest thing is just to start trying by every day doing something good for yourself that rejects the thinking of the popular culture. Each accomplishment is another brick in your new *House of Wisdom*. The more you embrace the change the easier it becomes and there is no looking back in the rear view mirror as it will only bring conflicting emotions that diminish the growth of these new positive energies.

Once you have illuminated yourself to this *thought platform* that is directed by your *Life Ethic, Guiding Logic and Compelling Passion* you will find that you possess some strong desire to answer the questions of your *Five Focal Facts*. In doing this there comes an even deeper understanding of your life, its meaning and your destiny. This **VisionQuest of Self** is not some obsessive compulsive activity but is part of your self-awareness and actually you will find that it will be your life experiences at certain junctures that will answer the five questions in a very natural manner.

All these cocktail of feelings and thoughts form your *Unified Life Philosophy* which is your compass and road map. This archetypal inspiration further develops the work-in-progress *Ultimate You* to possess a spring in your step, a song on your lips and an overwhelming desire to give, care and share with others. Through your cumulative actions your behavior becomes your *Trademark of Positivity*. This *Positivity* is your consistent *Signature Brand* that delights friends and greatly confounds adversaries.

Days becomes months, then years to decades, it is remarkable how fast thirty years can pass. Like the twinkle of any eye our footprint on this earth is here then gone but if you have been enjoying life doing good things that vast body of virtuous energy becomes much larger than you. It is from these consistent small day-by-day behaviors that legacies are created; usually much to the surprise of the humble hard-working people who accomplish them… their destiny was fulfilled in the simple silence of their good life.

Positivity is a state of *Mindfulness* that encompasses the *totality of our Intellectual and Emotional Self*. Positivity is the essence of the Spirit as it expresses *Love, Hope and Trust*. It is the *Ultimate Inspiration* that informs, educates and encourages the next generation with your bright wisdom. Positivity gives meaning to life as it desires to discover the spirit of divine creation which in our quest for purposeful meaning we seek to emulate.

This Invincible Optimism has been the genesis of innovation that has improved the quality of life for the entire world. If you seek to find improvement then you must become the change that you seek to find; for we have only one life to get this right!

# 7.

# Destiny

WHAT IS REALLY IMPORTANT? ... From our ten-thousand-mile journey of a hundred thousand footsteps, in which we encountered twenty-five thousand souls and lived on this Earth for almost five million moments, what wisdom did we gather and what wisdom will remain?

How many virtuous deeds become the light which created our wisdom? In the final measure it will not be the gold and silver that will carry us on our way, but *Who we are, What we did* and the footprint that remains of our essence... In light of these things did we use our time well and completely fulfilled the journey our destiny?

In thinking about one's destiny you must first start at the beginning where your story all began; reflecting upon the lessons of your youth. Fortunate is the individual who can live their entire life and never lose their child's heart. For in the idealistic purity of these hopeful dreams come powerful archetypal energies that connect us to the collective unconscious to inspire an adult life of creative lofty nurturing concepts.

This *Inner Voice* quietly reassures the youthful truths that beloved role models gave to enlivens us with their hope that we would continue that chain of their wisdom through our own personalized contribution to the next generation.

While the "Us" Culture lives the temporary life, the "We" Culture is most transcendent as it represents Past-Present-Future. We do live in the *Here- And-Now* but we also have our other foot firmly planted in building for tomorrow; for the future is where we are going to live.

The secret to a positive quality life is being centered in a stillness to be able to hear what your quiet *Inner Voice* is trying to say. The flashing roar of the "Us" Culture in its noisy nonsense distracts your unconscious energy from seeking *Active Balance*.

Healthy positive individuals have a place of reflection in their psyche that becomes the crucible for the archetypal energies of their child's heart. These archetypes lift their dreams upward and provide for a life of aspiration and to the spiritually minded a personalized access to transcendent energies far beyond our mortal ability to comprehend. This mystical, spiritual connection is *Tribal* in its linkage to past ancestors, active ministry to people in the present and future aspirations for the generations yet to come. It explains with such clarity the meaning of our life.

This **Aspirational Culture** is the launching pad of *Champions* who believe in the pursuit of dreams that are fueled by a vision. The very zeitgeist of the *American Psyche* is formed around this concept; the belief that hard-working virtue is the fulfillment of our individual and collective destiny... the *American Dream*.

While this does provide a large part of the foundation of our collective optimism it is further reinforced through the children's book we read in our youth. These stories of simple characters overcoming obstacles to win and achieve success; is the red meat that we all first cut our young teeth upon. Yet the stories were not solely about winning but through the pursuit of certain lofty principles; the good, positive and virtuous person would always prevail.

As much as there are those who choose to be jaded, ascribing these youthful myths as unrealistic fluff, there are equally those like myself that believe that these principles of the *"High Road"* are the very best of our collective culture. In fact they are the grist through the mill that created a culture of *Exceptionalism* that has been globally emulated.

I am connected to these myths from my youth that have served me well through a diversity of complex and difficult circumstances. It is impossible for me to debate their value as in the global circles that I have traveled their appeal is universal which only re-confirms for me the sustainable influence and wisdom of their message... the dream to aspire is indelible to the human spirit.

So with my child's heart and a pocket filled with my youthful myths I am able to rise above the cynicism of this age to believe that most people are very good. Their good nature is clouded by daily stress, disrupted by worry and distorted by the shallow distractions of the *Bread and Circus* "Us" Culture. Few people are bad by nature but many are lost, confused and searching for the answer.

Some would say this life philosophy is simplistic, extremely naïve and unsophisticated. Actually from my experience, in its simple effectiveness this philosophy is highly sophisticated as it produces consistent sustainable, excellence far superior to that of the "Us" Culture. It is a place of altruistic *Common Ground* where differences melt away for the unity of the human spirit's good intentions always finds a mutual *Positive Life Philosophy*.

These are just the practical elements of this *Positive Life Philosophy* that can be readily justified. Their more exponential value are the archetypal images that this positive philosophy inspires in your thinking, lifestyle, and achievements which creates the narrative for your exceptional beautiful life story.

It is these larger than life stories that are the seeds where legacies take root, grow and develop. These *Champion Leader Cultures* are places where *Heroes, Sages and Philosophers* re-tell our youthful stories again and again to instill these positive, affirming principles for our entire life. Is the alternative approach more beneficially life-affirming to your health, wealth and wisdom .. You Tell Me?

Achieving the *Journey of the Self* to fulfill our destiny requires this type of archetypal characters and stories for they give us a wider view of life and its ultimate purpose. To reject these *Archetypal Energies* is to live a superficial life of shallow temporary pleasures to find yourself in those last moments of life thinking about driving your favorite sports car instead of being filled with an abundance of uncontainable gratitude for a life well-lived in which you gave it your best portion every day to create something vast and far greater than yourself.

Living a good quality positive life of meaning requires some type of engagement with your spiritual dimension. Absent those experiences, every moment in your life is only about satisfying whatever pressing impulse that you feel without any consideration for its future collective impact. This *"Drive Through Lifestyle"* thinking is the great peril of our times and the source of such negative energy, confusion, illness and overwhelming general disruptive dissatisfaction.

The Ultimate Inspiration is to live the best quality life that is possible for you and to aspire every day to further enrich it for you possess a unique gift that must be shared with the entire world. Your life's journey is to express its many dimensions every day with joyful excitement. Your beautiful life is one that is fascinated and enthralled with other people whose warmth that you have inspired is the never-setting sunshine that becomes *Your Truth, Your Vision* and finally *Your Legacy* that will continue long after you have passed to your reward.

*You are a miracle that only once will come to this earth to share your unique gift with humanity.* It is your choice to be either a dark cloud that blocks out the sunshine or to be the sunshine that sparkles above far beyond all the clouds; as a bright beacon of a Positive Life......

Yes: You are the Ultimate Inspiration!